HOW TO RUN A SUCCESSFUL SUPERMARKET

Step-by-Step Guide

By Ekwulo C. John

DEDICATION

This book is dedicated to my mum Mrs Caroline Ekwulo, and my mentor
they contributed greatly to my broad knowledge in business field

CONTENTS

INTRODUCTION:

Greetings and thanks for visiting "How to Run a Successful Supermarket: A Comprehensive Guide." This eBook is created to give you useful insights and hands-on expertise knowledge about setting up and managing a successful supermarket, whether you're a driven entrepreneur, an aspiring business owner, or simply intrigued by the world of retail.

We will examine the crucial components of establishing your own supermarket chapter by chapter, equipping you with the knowledge and skills required to negotiate the complex retail landscape and start a fruitful entrepreneurial adventure. Let's examine the importance of this undertaking, the difficulties it poses, and the benefits it offers.

Importance of setting up a grocery store:

A grocery shop serves many purposes than merely providing access to everyday supplies and food. It functions as a crucial center among communities, satisfying a basic need by giving easy access to necessities. Your grocery shop will play a significant part in your customers' lives, contributing to their well-being and ingraining itself firmly into their daily routines.

Discuss the potential rewards and difficulties briefly:

Opening a supermarket has many perks and challenges. Making wise decisions requires awareness of potential roadblocks. Intense rivalry, shifting consumer preferences, and the necessity for efficient inventory management are a few potential obstacles. The benefits, however, are just as promising, including developing a successful business, producing job possibilities, and having a positive influence on the neighborhood. Now, let's look at the road map that will lead you through the book's chapters:

Learn the value of market research, how to define your target market, and how to write a sound business plan to build a solid foundation for your grocery shop.

Recognize the essential elements in choosing the best position to guarantee accessibility, closeness to residential regions, and compliance with zoning and regulatory regulations.

Learn how to design an appealing and practical store layout, organize products optimally, and include effective checkout and payment methods to improve the entire shopping experience.

Supplier sourcing and Inventory Management: Dive into the strategies for sourcing reliable suppliers, building relationships with local farmers, distributors, producers, and implementing effective inventory management systems to ensure a consistent supply of High-quality products.

Staffing and Training: Gain insights into determining staffing needs, hiring competent employees, and providing comprehensive training to deliver exceptional customer service and product knowledge.

Technology and Systems: Explore the utilization of technology, such as point-of-sale (POS) systems, inventory management software, and accounting systems, to streamline operations, enhance efficiency, and drive growth. Financial accounting and filing system: Learn essential tips on record keeping following generally accepted accounting principles (GAAP). How to trace transactions and identify errors, both intentional and accidental. Marketing and Advertising: Develop a comprehensive marketing strategy, utilizing various channels to understanding the significance of store aesthetics, cleanliness, and easy services will help you establish an environment that encourages customer happiness, loyalty, and continuous patronage.

Recap the main ideas covered in the eBook, inspire would-be grocery store owners, and provide some last-minute advice and reminders for success in opening and operating a grocery shop.

You will have a thorough understanding of the complexities involved in opening a grocery shop by the time this eBook is over, and you will be armed with the information and direction need to start your own business with confidence.

Let's start by reading the first chapter, "Market Research and Planning," to establish the groundwork for your prosperous grocery store.

MARKET RESEARCH AND PLANNING

Detailed market analysis and extensive business planning are two of the most important steps in starting your food shop. The four main components of market research and planning—understanding your target market, evaluating the local competitors, completing feasibility studies, and creating an effective business plan—are covered in this chapter.

Finding your target market: Knowing and understanding your target market is crucial for the establishment and expansion of your grocery shop. Analyze local demographics, consumer trends, and shopping habits. Age groups, financial levels, lifestyle choices, and cultural variety should all be taken into account. You can use this knowledge to modify your product offers, marketing tactics, and retail atmosphere to meet the needs of the target market.

Conducting market research and feasibility studies:

Market research and feasibility studies are essential to assessing the viability and potential success of your grocery store. This involves gathering data on market size, growth projections, consumer trends, and industry dynamics. Conduct surveys, interviews, and focus groups to gather insights directly from potential customers. Additionally, assess the feasibility of your grocery store by analyzing factors such as costs, location, infrastructure, and regulatory requirements. Feasibility studies will help you make informed decisions about the viability of your business concept and identify potential risks and challenges.

A well-developed business plan is a roadmap for the success of your grocery store. It outlines your vision, mission, goals, and strategies. Include sections such as an executive summary, company description, market analysis, competitive analysis, product offerings, marketing and sales strategies, operational plan, financial projections, and risk management. A comprehensive business plan not only serves as a guide for you but also helps attract potential investors or secure financing from banks or lending institutions.

By dedicating time and effort to market research and planning, you will gain valuable insights that will inform critical decisions in the setup and operation of your grocery store. Understanding your target market, assessing competition, conducting feasibility studies, and creating a well-crafted business plan will lay the foundation for a successful and sustainable grocery store. Now that you have a strong understanding of market research and planning, let's move forward to Chapter 3: Choosing the Right Location. This chapter will guide you through the process of selecting the optimal location for your grocery store, ensuring maximum visibility, accessibility, and convenience for your target audience.

CHOOSING THE RIGHT LOCATION

When it comes to setting up a grocery store, selecting the

right location is a crucial decision that can significantly

impact the success of your business. In this chapter, we will

delve into the key considerations for choosing the optimal

location for your grocery store. We will explore factors to consider, evaluate population density and demographics, assess proximity to residential areas transportation, and understand zoning and regulatory requirements. By thoroughly analyzing these elements, you can make an informed decision that aligns with your target market and sets your grocery store up for success.

Factors to consider when selecting a location:

Choosing the right location involves evaluating various factors that can directly influence your grocery store's performance. Some key considerations include: Visibility: Opt for a location that offers high visibility, preferably on main roads or in areas with heavy foot and vehicle traffic. A prominent location increases the chances of attracting customers and generating awareness for your store. Accessibility: Ensure your grocery store is easily accessible to customers. Consider the convenience of both motorists and pedestrians and evaluate their proximity to major roads, highways, public transportation, and parking facilities.

Competition: Assess the presence and proximity of existing grocery stores and supermarkets in the area. While some competition can indicate a viable market, too much saturation may pose challenges. Look for locations where you can differentiate your offerings and target underserved segments. Surrounding Businesses: Consider the types of businesses in the vicinity of the potential location. Look for complementary businesses that can drive foot traffic, such as pharmacies, bakeries, or coffee shops. Avoid areas with businesses that directly compete with your product offerings.

Evaluating population density and demographics:

Understanding the local population is crucial for tailoring

your grocery store to their needs. Evaluate the population density and demographics of the surrounding area, including factors such as age groups, income levels, family sizes, and cultural diversity. This information helps determine the range of products and services you should offer, pricing strategies, and marketing approaches that resonate with your target customers. Assessing proximity to residential areas and transportation: Proximity to residential areas is key to a grocery store's success. Look for locations in close proximity to residential neighborhoods, apartment complexes, or housing developments. Being conveniently located near customers' homes reduces travel time and encourages frequent visits. Additionally, assess the accessibility of the location in terms of transportation options. Consider the presence of bus stops, train stations, or major roadways to ensure easy access for customer.

Understanding zoning and regulatory requirements:

Before finalizing a location, it is crucial to understand the zoning regulations and other regulatory requirements that may impact your grocery store. Research local ordinances and regulations related to permits, licenses, signage, parking restrictions, and operating hours. Compliance with these regulations is essential for a smooth operation and to avoid legal complications down the line. By carefully considering these factors and conducting thorough research, you can select a location that aligns with your target market, offers convenience to customers and complies with local regulations. A strategic location sets the foundation for attracting customers, building loyalty, and ensuring the long-term success of your grocery store.

In the next chapter, "Store Layout and Design," we will explore how to create an attractive and functional layout for your grocery store, optimize product placement, and enhance the overall shopping experience.

In the next chapter, "Store Layout and Design," we will explore how to create an attractive and functional layout for your grocery store, optimize product placement, and enhance the overall shopping experience.

STORE LAYOUT AND DESIGN

The layout and design of your grocery store play a significant role in attracting customers, enhancing their shopping experience, and maximizing sales. In this chapter, we will explore the key aspects of store layout and design. We will discuss determining the size and layout of your store, creating an attractive and functional store design, optimizing

product placement and aisle organization, and incorporating efficient checkout and payment systems. By carefully considering these elements, you can create a grocery store that is visually appealing, easy to navigate, and optimized for customer satisfaction.

Determining the size and layout of your store:

The size and layout of your grocery store will depend on various factors, including available space, target market, and product range. Consider the flow of customer traffic, aisle width, and space allocation for different departments such as produce, meat, dairy, and dry goods. Optimize the store layout to ensure efficient movement and easy access to products. Additionally, allocate space creating an attractive and functional store design: An attractive store design is essential for creating a welcoming and pleasant shopping environment. Consider the overall aesthetic, color scheme, lighting, and signage. Choose a design that aligns with your brand identity and appeals to your target market. A well-designed store can create a positive first impression, encourage customers to explore the aisles, and increase their likelihood of making purchases.

Optimizing product placement and aisle organization:

Strategic product placement and aisle organization are crucial for maximizing sales and improving the shopping experience. Place high-demand items and essential products in easily accessible areas, such as near the entrance or checkout counters. Organize aisles logically, grouping similar products together and considering customer flow patterns. Use clear signage and shelf labels to help customers find products quickly. Regularly review and update the layout based on customer feedback and purchasing trends.

Incorporating efficient checkout and payment systems:

Minimizing consumer wait times and offering a seamless checkout experience depend on effective checkout and payment systems. Based on the expected consumer volume, think about where to locate the checkout counters. To make the checkout process faster, use barcode scanners, POS (point-of-sale) software, and integrated payment methods. Staff members should receive training on how to use the devices effectively and offer timely, courteous customer care when customers are checking out.

You may build a grocery shop that is aesthetically pleasing, well-organized, and practical for customers by carefully taking into account the size, layout, design, product placement, and checkout systems. The overall shopping experience is improved and customers are enticed to spend more time browsing and making purchases when a store is well-designed.

Experience and encourages customers to spend more time exploring and purchasing products.

We will go over how to find dependable suppliers, set up effective inventory management systems, and guarantee product quality and variety in your grocery shop in the subsequent chapter, "supplier sourcing," to be published soon.

SUPPLIER SOURCING

Choosing the right suppliers is essential to opening a profitable grocery business. We will explore the crucial factors for choosing trustworthy suppliers and distributors in this chapter, as well as how to establish connections with regional farmers and producers. You can give your consumers a wide choice of alternatives and guarantee a consistent supply of high-quality products for your grocery shop by building strong supplier networks.

Identifying reliable suppliers and distributors:

Finding trustworthy and dependable suppliers and distributors is the first step in the supplier sourcing process. When assessing potential suppliers, keep the following things in mind:

Product Quality: Look for vendors who can regularly deliver

goods of a high caliber that satisfy your store's requirements. For a complete evaluation of their products, do extensive research, read customer testimonials, and ask for samples.

Pricing and payment terms: To identify the most affordable solutions, evaluate the pricing plans and payment schedules offered by various suppliers. Take into account elements like credit terms, volume discounts, and delivery schedules. While some vendors prefer an immediate payment, others will take a credit facility for 1-2 weeks. You can lessen supplier power during the negotiation and make it a fixed package for all transactions with them depending on the standard to which you create your shop. Don't treat all suppliers equally when negotiating payment arrangements; a supplier who offers products with a high turnover rate might not be willing to be flexible with payments. However, new suppliers or those providing goods that are untested in the market ought to be given sale or return payment terms

(SOR). This is due to the likelihood that the products will result in a slow return on profit (ROP).

Timeliness and dependability: Ensure that vendors have a track record of providing goods on schedule and in full. Customer dissatisfaction may result from delayed deliveries or variable stock availability can lead to customer dissatisfaction and affect your store's reputation.

Geographic proximity: Take into account where the store's suppliers are located. Working with local or regional vendors can have benefits including cheaper shipping, quicker delivery, and the option to purchase locally produced, fresh goods.

Supplier Relationships: Look into the reputation of the supplier within the sector and their connections to other merchants. Select vendors with a solid track record of professionalism, responsiveness, and cooperation.

Establishing connections with nearby farmers and producers:

For your grocery shop, establishing connections with regional farmers and producers can have several advantages. You can create these links in the following ways:

Farmers markets and neighborhood events are great places to meet and network with local farmers and producers. Talk to them to learn about their products, farming methods, and production capacities.

Visit local farms to learn more about their operations, product offerings, and quality assurance procedures. Developing a personal connection with farmers can increase trust and make direct sourcing easier.

Cooperative Associations: Become a member of regional or local organizations that connect farmers and producers. These organizations frequently have networks or directories that can put you in touch with reputable vendors in your area

Engage with the neighborhood by taking part in neighborhood activities or supporting neighborhood projects. Through your participation, you can build relationships with farmers and producers and demonstrate your dedication to assisting small businesses in your community.

Community Engagement: Investigate the possibilities of making contractual agreements with producers and farmers.

This can provide stability and a consistent supply of fresh, seasonal crops. And support local agricultural communities.

Contract Farming: By identifying reliable suppliers and distributors, and building relationships with local farmers and producers, you can secure a diverse range of high-quality products for your grocery store. These partnerships can also contribute to a sense of community and sustainability, which can resonate with your customers and differentiate your store from competitors.

We will cover how to create effective inventory management systems in the following chapter, "Inventory Management," to guarantee product freshness, diversity, and ideal stock levels in your grocery shop.

INVENTORY MANAGEMENT

A grocery business needs effective inventory management in order to run smoothly. In this chapter, we'll look at the important factors to take into account while setting up effective inventory management systems, maintaining product quality, freshness, and diversity, and putting in place a checkpoint system for product security. You can minimize stock outs, cut waste, and offer a wide selection of high-quality products to your clients by improving your inventory management procedures.

1. Implementing effective inventory management techniques: Implementing tools and procedures to efficiently track, manage, and refill your store's inventory is a key component of good inventory management. Think about the following tactics:

• Inventory Tracking: Utilize inventory management software or POS systems with inventory tracking capabilities. These tools can help you monitor stock levels, track sales data, and generate reports for informed decision-making.

• Forecasting demand: To produce an accurate forecast, use past sales information, seasonal patterns, and consumer preferences. This makes it possible for you to minimize the danger of having too much or too little stock by adjusting inventory levels and ordering quantities accordingly.

• Just-in-Time (JIT) Methodology: Utilize a just-in-time inventory strategy by placing orders for products to arrive just before consumption. This tactic lowers carrying expenses and lessens the possibility of product deterioration.

• Stock Replenishment: To ensure prompt replenishment, set up automatic reorder points depending on inventory levels. Review sales data often to spot hot and cold commodities, altering reorder quantities and intervals accordingly.

2. Ensuring the freshness, variety, and quality of the products: Maintaining product quality, freshness, and

diversity is crucial for customer satisfaction and loyalty. Consider the following methods:

• Supplier Connections: Develop trusting connections with suppliers who place a high priority on quality control. Keep in touch with your suppliers on a regular basis to learn about product availability, freshness, and any potential problems.

• FIFO (First-In, First-Out): Use the FIFO method of product rotation, whereby older stock is sold ahead of fresh stock. This minimizes waste and guarantees freshness by guaranteeing that products are sold prior to their expiration dates. A good way to reduce losses is to train both new and experienced staff to stack products in front of older products or to sell off older products.

• Quality Assurance Checks: Regularly inspect products upon delivery to ensure they meet quality standards. Monitor expiration dates, packaging integrity, and overall product condition. Establish protocols for handling and removing expired or damaged items from the sales floor promptly.

• Seasonal and Local Offerings: To give clients variety and encourage community support, introduce seasonal and locally sourced products. To acquire fresh and distinctive products, work directly with regional farmers, producers, and suppliers.

3. Establishing a checkpoint mechanism for product security: For the purpose of protecting goods, minimizing theft, and keeping correct inventory records, a checkpoint system is essential. Think about these techniques:

° Costs and markup: Markup in Grocery Stores

The practice of raising the price of goods sold in a grocery store over their wholesale or cost price is known as grocery store price markup. This markup is used to produce a profit for the store and pay for other expenses. Even though the precise markup percentage can change depending on the shop, the area, and the goods, it is a widely used practice in retail industry.

There are several factors that contribute to the price markup in grocery stores. Let's explore some of the key factors:

Grocery businesses, like any other business, have operating expenditures such as rent, utilities, employee compensation, insurance, and upkeep. These costs must be met by the markup on items. For instance, a store in a desirable area with high rent prices might have to charge a higher markup to cover those costs.

Groceries must be moved from suppliers to the store and stored in the proper manner during transportation and storage. Transportation expenditures, such as fuel, delivery trucks, and logistics, increase overall prices. Furthermore, suitable storage facilities, such as refrigeration for perishable items, necessitate investment. These expenses are reflected in the markup. As a business-minded individual, you must keep in mind all of these elements and remember that high sales turnover is preferable to high profit. So, when deciding on the optimal markup for your products, keep in mind that the provision section is where you make the most sales, and clients will always utilize this section to compare your prices to competitors' rates. The most effective technique to draw them into your store is to apply a markup of 10–20% to both domestic and foreign goods. Drinks are a highly popular category, so you may bargain with suppliers and purchase goods for a minimal markup. When you acquire it cheaply, you can sell it. Make sure you allow clients to buy products with pack discounts so that you can sell more because they will have access to wholesale prices. The wine department markup should be between 25-30% for all alcoholic beverages.

Inventory Management-selling stores must properly manage their inventory to provide a consistent supply of products. This entails monitoring inventory levels, cutting waste, and controlling expiration dates. To account for probable losses and the work associated with inventory management, a markup is imposed to preserve profitability.

Supplier Relationships: Grocery stores negotiate costs with suppliers to acquire the products they require. They must take into account the necessity to turn a profit while still attempting to secure the greatest wholesale costs. The markup aids in bridging the gap between the wholesale price and the retail price.

Competition and Market Demand: Market considerations such as competition and customer demand influence a food store's pricing approach. Stores must set pricing that is competitive in their local market while also remaining profitable. When a product is in high demand, the retailer may decide to reduce the markup to draw customers in or even sell it below cost to draw people in and promote more purchases.

Profit Margin: In the end, supermarkets are businesses that want to turn a profit. The price markup generates income that covers all of the aforementioned costs and allows for a healthy profit margin. Depending on the store's business model, target market, and overall financial objectives, the precise markup percentage may change.

It's significant to remember that not all items in grocery stores have the same markup. Items in high demand or those that require specialized handling (e.g., organic vegetables) may have a greater markup than staple products or those in low demand.

While consumers may occasionally discover that the markup on grocery store products is higher than what they would pay at a wholesale or bulk merchant, it is critical to consider the convenience, variety, and other services given by grocery stores. These elements enhance the whole shopping experience and may help certain shoppers understand the price difference.

• Controlled Access: Limit access to storage spaces and

ensure that only authorized staff members handle goods. To protect precious or high-risk items, use lockable storage cabinets, cages, or limited spaces.

Radio Frequency Identification (RFID) is a technology that uses radio waves to identify and track things or persons. It is made up of three major parts: RFID tags, RFID readers, and a backend system. The RFID tags, which can either be active or passive (powered by the reader's signal), store data or transmit it when the reader's signal activates the tags. Readers emit radio waves that interact with the tags and collect the information they contain. A backend uses this information once it has been processed.

The system can be incorporated into a variety of applications such as inventory management, access control, supply chain tracking, and others. RFID technology provides benefits like real-time tracking, automation, and increased efficiency in a variety of industries. The use of RFID technology in a store to regulate the flow of merchandise and lower stealing. People pick up new shoplifting techniques as the world evolves. You must improve your expertise as a business owner by studying fresh methods to protect your stock, like this RFID technology. You can contact me at 07085884934 for inquiries related to installing this system in your store.

A grocery store's "human checkpoint" is often a manned section where staff members keep an eye on and help customers. This can entail duties like checking IDs for items with age restrictions, helping consumers use self-checkpoint, answering queries, or making sure that patrons abide by store policies. This checkpoint system can be used to securely and cost-effectively regulate inventories. Unlike the RFID technology system, which is an automated checkpoint that saves money, this human checkpoint system provides a personal touch to the shopping experience and aids in efficient business operations. This process requires a check point officer to be designated to wait at the exit door point and examine customer's and employee's receipts as they leave the store, the procedure works as intended. This procedure should be followed for goods received in the store, both local supplies and general market purchase. Two or more employees should be assigned to control this task, it's imperative for products to be checked by a minimum of two people to ensure the sincerity in products received process. Their role in restock process is to receive products by picking out products listed in each invoice with an accounting pen either red or green. This way all products that were not supplied from the purchase would be identified and retrieved from the market. But small store, one person can be in charge of the checking of receipt the second person will be the inventory manager. So any error that the checking officer does not identify, the inventory will identify the product. And most importantly in this process the checking officers must pay attention to expiry date, and the inventory officer needs to look closely at the expiry while entering the products.

Employee training: Inform staff members on how to manage inventory correctly, including examining new shipments, performing routine stock counts, and reporting discrepancies. Create processes for reporting and investigating alleged thefts or stockpile losses. Establish procedures for reporting and looking into alleged thefts or inventory losses.

Install video cameras in key locations to monitor storage areas and deter theft. Ensure that there is enough signage warning employees and customers about the presence of surveillance systems.

Setting up an inventory management system, ensuring product quality, freshness, and variety, and building a checkpoint system for securing products will help you maintain appropriate stock levels, reduce waste, and provide your customers with a wonderful shopping experience.

Product stacking: This action is necessary to boost sales and requires this step to be taken. To maintain product visibility and accessibility, a grocery shop must adhere to a number of stacking regulations.

Similar goods might be stacked together to provide buyers with the opportunity to test new products. Although not all items respond well to this method, it has been demonstrated

to significantly increase sales and aid in the adoption of new

products.

Implementing a Planogram: Planograms are diagrams that show how items should be arranged on shelves. They increase visibility, make shelves more efficient, and make sure that goods are attractively displayed.

Product display visibility: A product that is visible to customers will generate sales. Some customers enter a store without having a clear idea of the specific item they wish to learn more about. Because consumers will only buy items they can see, products that are more visible sell better. Take into consideration the illustration's example. Customers may easily stroll up to this shelf and make their selection due to its high visibility.

In the following chapter, "Staffing and Training," we will cover how to determine staffing needs, locate and hire competent personnel, and establish training programs to ensure excellent customer service and product knowledge in your grocery shop. Look closely at the illustration below; you'll see that similar detergents are Take a close look at the image below to see how identical detergents are piled next to each other. Customers can readily make their choice considering price disparities and quality with the manner they were stacked? This approach works well for emerging and successful products. When products are stacked in this manner, a client may purchase more products since they may have budgeted for detergent, and when they see different varieties, the desire to purchase the new variety will arise.

STAFFING AND TRAINING

You must have an experienced and driven workforce for your grocery business to succeed. The essential factors for hiring and educating employees will be addressed in this chapter, including identifying staffing needs and positions, finding qualified candidates, employing them, putting them through customer service and product knowledge training, and putting performance evaluation and incentives in place. By putting money into your employees and giving them the training and resources they need, you can foster a healthy work atmosphere and provide your clients with outstanding service.

1. Determining staff requirements and roles: Take into account elements like store size, customer traffic, and the range of products you sell when figuring out your workforce needs. A flawless operation depends on a number of critical positions, including cashiers, (procurement officers) stock replenishes, department supervisors, inventory officers, and customer service representatives. Based on peak and off-peak hours, determine the ideal staffing ratio for each position, and provide detailed job descriptions and expectations.

2. Finding and appointing qualified personnel finding qualified personnel who share the goals and values of your company requires efficient recruitment and hiring procedures. Think about the following tactics:

• Employment Postings: Post-employment openings on job boards, in local publications, or on the website of your business. Give a detailed breakdown of each role's prerequisites, experience, and duties. To increase your reach, make use of social media sites and online professional connections. Employing experienced workers will increase the value of your company because they will comprehend your training more easily and contribute their prior experience. However, it's crucial to give novice staff members excellent training to increase efficiency.

• Application and Interview Process: Develop a tough application process that includes collecting resumes, cover letters, and references. Conduct structured interviews to assess candidates' skills, experience, and suitability for the role. Consider conducting practical assessments or scenario-based exercises to evaluate their abilities in a grocery store environment.

• Measure the candidates' cultural fit with your store's values and culture during the interview process. Look for people who have a strong work ethic, a love for helping others, and the capacity to function well in a team.

• Checks of the Past: To verify the honesty and dependability of new employees, run background investigations, including reference checks and, if necessary, criminal record checks.

3. Educating personnel on product expertise and customer service: For providing a satisfying shopping experience, thorough training in customer service and product expertise is essential. Take into account the following training

techniques:

• Orientation: Offer a thorough orientation program to introduce new hires to the policies, practices, and values of your store. Describe them and explain what their responsibilities are and what you expect of them.

• Product Training: Educate your workers thoroughly about the goods you sell. Introduce them to the benefits, features, and safe handling of the product. Encourage lifelong learning and inform personnel of alterations and new product releases.

• Customer Service Training: Offer instruction on good customer service techniques, such as active listening, problem-solving, and addressing client enquiries or complaints. Stress the value of having a welcoming and accommodating approach towards consumers.

Offer staff role-specific training to make sure they are aware of their duties and obligations. Provide instruction on safe operating practices, stock management, cashier processes, and department-specific activities.4.   Implementing performance evaluation and incentives: Regular performance evaluation and incentives can motivate and reward your employees. Consider these practices:

•   Performance Reviews: Conduct regular performance reviews to provide feedback on employees' strengths and areas for improvement. Set goals and objectives to guide their professional development. Offer constructive feedback and recognize their achievements.

•   Incentive Programs: Implement incentive programs such as performance bonuses, recognition programs, or employee-of-the-month awards. These programs can boost morale and motivate staff to excel in their roles.

•   Ongoing Training and Development: Encourage

continuous learning and skill development by offering opportunities for training and workshops. Support employees who show interest in expanding their knowledge or taking on additional responsibilities.

Continuous Training and Development: Promote skill improvement and learning by providing chances for training and workshops. Encourage staff members who express a desire to learn more or assume more responsibility.

• Team-building exercises Create social or team-building events to promote a supportive and cohesive workplace culture. Encourage open communication, teamwork, and teamwork among your staff members.

You can create a competent and motivated team that contributes to the success of your grocery store by identifying the staffing needs and roles, finding and employing competent employees, training them in customer service and product knowledge, and putting performance evaluation and incentives in place. Call me at 07085884934 if you need employee training that is either one-on-one or online.

"Technology and Systems," we will discuss the importance of leveraging technology in your grocery store, including choosing and implementing a point-of-sale system, utilizing inventory management software, and leveraging technology for marketing and customer engagement.

TECHNOLOGY AND SYSTEMS

Utilizing technology is crucial for a food store's successful operation in the modern digital world. The significance of technology and systems will be discussed in this chapter, with a particular emphasis on four key areas: selecting and implementing a point-of-sale (POS) system, using inventory management software, implementing efficient accounting and bookkeeping systems, and utilizing technology for marketing and customer engagement. By utilizing technology, you may improve productivity, streamline processes, and give your customers an effortless shopping experience.

Choosing and implementing a point-of-sale (POS) system:

A robust POS system is the backbone of your store's operations. Consider the following when choosing and implementing a POS system:

Functionality: Select a point-of-sale system that provides essential functions including barcode scanning, inventory management, sales tracking, and reporting. Check to see if it interfaces with other software and systems you intend to utilize.

User-Friendliness: Pick a system that is simple to understand and use so that your team can use it efficiently. Take into account the POS system provider's support and training programmes.

Scalability: Take into account the future growth and expansion plans for your store. Make sure the POS system can handle a rise in transaction volume as well as any additional features or locations that may be required.

Payment Options: Look for a POS system that supports various payment methods, including credit and debit cards, mobile payments, and digital wallets, to offer convenience to your customers.

Utilizing inventory management software:

A potent tool for reducing inventory-related processes, tracking product movement, and optimizing stock levels is inventory management software. When selecting inventory management software, take into account the following advantages and features:

Tracking in real-time: To keep track of stock levels, follow product movement, and get low-stock warnings, look for software that offers real-time inventory updates. Stock shortages and overstocking are reduced as a result. Although retailers utilize a lot of software, not all of it provides sufficient data for effective product control. Knowing reliable software with sufficient data is advantageous since it puts you on the right path to maximizing profits. However, if you want to get in touch with me by WhatsApp or phone, my number is 07085884934.

Supplier Integration: Choose software that integrates with your suppliers' systems, enabling seamless communication and automated inventory replenishment. This reduces manual effort and improves accuracy.

Software that offers reports on sales and demand analysis should be sought out. You may use these insights to inform your data-driven decisions about ordering products, running promotions, and maximizing your inventory.

Barcode Scanning: Select software with barcode scanning capabilities to improve the accuracy and efficiency of inventory management.

Putting in place efficient bookkeeping and accounting

systems:

For controlling cash flow, keeping track of spending, and maintaining compliance, proper accounting and bookkeeping systems are crucial. Think about the following techniques:

Accounting programmes Invest in accounting software that makes duties like documenting sales, monitoring spending, handling payroll, and generating financial reports easier to manage. For easy data synchronization, pick software that integrates with your point-of-sale system.

Create a thorough chart of accounts that is suited to the unique requirements of your food store. This will help organize and categorize income, expenses, and assets. Cash Flow Management: Implement effective cash flow management practices, including preserving adequate working capital, keeping an eye on cash flow data, and controlling vendor payment terms.

Internal financial controls should be put in place to protect against fraud and maintain accurate financial records. This can entail setting up mechanisms for purchasing orders, carrying out routine audits, and separating financial tasks.

Utilizing technology for marketing and customer interaction: Technology presents several chances for efficiently promoting your grocery shop and interacting with customers. Think about the following tactics:

Online Visibility: To showcase your shop, advertise special deals, and interact with customers on social media, develop a good website and keep active social media profiles. To increase online visibility, use search engine optimize (SEO) strategies.

Create a client email list and regularly send newsletters or promotional emails to this list to inform customers about new products, deals, and events. Email personalization can increase consumer engagement.

Implement a consumer loyalty programme employing technology, such as a mobile app or digital loyalty card. To encourage repeat business and foster client loyalty, provide incentives like rewards, discounts, or special deals.

CRM (Customer Relationship Management) Systems: Use CRM software to compile customer information and preferences, enabling you to tailor marketing campaigns and deliver focused promotions.

You may improve operations, inventory management, financial records accuracy, marketing, and customer engagement at your grocery shop by adopting technology and putting the correct systems in place. If you will like to use a recommended and well-developed software for grocery store management you can reach out to me on 07085884934

In the next chapter, "Marketing and Advertising," we will delve deeper into developing a comprehensive marketing strategy, utilizing traditional and digital marketing channels, creating a brand identity, and fostering community engagement to attract and retain customers.

FINANCIAL ACCOUNTING AND FILING SYSTEM

I.   No matter the size of the firm, accounting is essential. The accounting system is what determines whether a food store will prosper or fail. Before a grocery store opens, the accounting system needs to be correctly configured to close all gaps in order for the business to be profitable. These gaps are mostly found at the points where goods are recognized as having been received (for purchases and restocking) and where cash is recognized as having been received (for cash point). These two points must be carefully monitored and structured to secure the shop. Nevertheless, there are other potential sources of revenue loss for a store, such as bank and expired goods. This is always easily tracked and monitored. This section will highlight several books and the steps that must be taken to secure the store. Effective efforts are taken to regulate the accounting process and important tactics for closing accounting loopholes are prevented; these strategies are crucial for minimizing losses.

II.   I. The recording of sales and revenue is the foundation of grocery store accounting. A sale must be documented regardless of whether it is paid for with cash, credit, or an electronic transfer.

Sales information reveals consumer preferences, best-selling items, and busiest shopping times. Regular study of this data improves marketing strategies and inventory management. When it is carefully monitored, a drop in sales will be found and recorded. For operational and financial reasons, accurate inventory tracking is essential. An efficient inventory management system keeps track of the things that are received, sold, and still have stock. By providing this knowledge, overstocking is avoided, waste is minimized, and customers are always able to purchase popular items.

III. Expense Monitoring Rent, utilities, employee pay, and other expenses are all part of running a grocery business. Payroll Management Employee wages are a significant the expense for any grocery store. Proper payroll management involves accurately calculating wages, and accounting for taxes, benefits, and overtime. Integrated payroll systems simplify this procedure and guarantee adherence to labor regulations.

Maintaining accurate records is the first step to effective food business accounting. It is crucial to have complete records of all financial transactions. This covers any other financial transactions as well as sales receipts, purchase invoices, expense receipts, and payroll records. These documents constitute the basis for evaluating the store's financial situation and coming to wise conclusions.

Efficient Filing Systems

By using a proper filling pattern for your shop, you may minimize revenue loss and improve document accessibility. The filling mechanism that would be more effective for your store depending on its size. While a mega store will require various filing lockers with separate compartments for each branch store, a small filing system for each location may be appropriate for a small business. This is true for grocery stores that plan to implement a central filing system.

In the fast-paced world of grocery retail, where success depends on customer happiness and operational effectiveness, efficiency is crucial. An efficient file system is one of the main factors that makes work more efficient. A well-structured filing system not only streamlines day-to-day operations but also ensures that customers can find products quickly, leading to a seamless shopping experience. In this article, we delve into the importance of filing systems in grocery stores and explore various strategies for creating and maintaining an effective filing system.

Importance of Filing Systems in Grocery Stores

A filing system in a grocery store serves as the backbone of the organization and facilitates a range of functions, including inventory management, restocking, and pricing. Some of the key reasons highlighting the significance of an efficient filing system are:

Document Accessibility: A well-organized filing system enables store employees to quickly locate invoice and other collectibles files for restocking and assists suppliers in finding invoices for unpaid transactions. This accessibility saves time for both supplier and staff, leading to a more pleasant transaction.

Inventory Management: An effective filing system aids in tracking inventory levels accurately. With categorized sections and proper labeling, staff can monitor stock levels and identify items that need restocking or have reached their expiration dates.

Time and Labor Savings: Efficient filing systems reduce the time spent searching for documents, thereby increasing the overall productivity of employees. This translates into lower labor costs and improved customer service.

Pricing and Promotion Management: Store managers may

keep track of pricing information and unique promotions with the aid of a structured filing system. This avoids pricing mistakes and guarantees uniformity throughout the store.

Techniques for a Successful Filing System

Planning carefully and paying attention to details are essential when creating an effective filing system. Here are some tactics to take into account:

Sort products into comprehensible categories, such as dairy, produce, meat, baked goods, canned goods, and so forth. Both staff and customers benefit from the search process being made simpler by categorization.

Put the products in alphabetical order inside each category. Customers and workers can find products more quickly as a result.

Product Codes and Barcodes: Give each item a special product code or barcode. At the point of sale, these codes can be scanned to aid inventory management.

Clear Labelling: For each area and shelf, use labels that are clear and succinct. The category name and any applicable subcategories should be included on labels, which should also be readable from a distance. You can label the file with a detailed description of the documents inside by using the large file envelope. Every day's bills are stapled inside the file and arranged according to how they come in each day, just to know the file below is labelled with the year 2020. If a store chooses to use the central filing system, each branch's locker may be identified, and all invoices can be arranged chronologically after being sorted.

For the store's filing system, two distinct files must be made for paid and outstanding bills. The file for unpaid invoices should have the label unpaid invoices clearly visible, and the file for paid invoices should have the label paid invoice visible. All paid invoices must be attached to and placed in a book titled Paid Invoices for a Store with Few Invoices, Paid Invoices for a Day. The clear document file may be helpful, depending on how many invoices need to be filed.

Continual Upkeep: Review and update the file system on a regular basis. To keep the system operating effectively as products evolve or new invoices are added, make the necessary adjustments.

Employee Education: Educate staff members thoroughly on the file system so they are aware of its layout and capable of assisting customers effectively. Technology Integration: Consider using electronic systems to track inventory, comparing invoices, to recorded purchase and expenses payments in sales analysis book. Invoices retrieved can compared to the invoices posted on system to ensure the information's recorded tally with the invoices on the system. This can enhance accuracy and streamline the ordering process.

The foundation of a good grocery shop business is an efficient filing system. It improves overall efficiency, increases supplier satisfaction and transparency, and optimizes inventory control. Grocery store owners and managers may create a seamless shopping experience that benefits both consumers and employees by putting into practice tactics like classification, clear labelling, and routine maintenance. Investing in a well-organized filing system is a calculated choice that pays off in the long term in a competitive retail environment.

Important accounting records: Store source documents are helpful in gathering accounting data from cashiers and inventories. Books like the supply register, cashier remission book, cashier submission book for chief cashiers, daily sales analysis book for chief cashier sales records, and costs book and payment book.

Restock book: The book is used by the inventory person to record all invoices received as hard copy, it picks information like restock date, invoice name, invoice number, product name, quantity supplied, amount, cost price, and selling price. This log book help to trace transactions of goods receipt and how they were entered in the system. The picture attached below, should be ruled in a hard notebook.

Date: 6th January, 2020				
Invoice name COCA-COLA BOTTLING COMPANY				
PRODUCT NAME	PRODUCT QTY	AMOUNT	COST PRICE	SELLING PRICE
COKE 50CL	12	1800	150	180
FANTA 50CL	120	18000	150	180
TOTAL		19800		

Cashier Submission: This book is the chief cashier sales record for POS, transfer, and cash remitted. This book is used by the chief cashier as a log book to record all sales information from cashiers. The picture below shows a template of a cashier submission.

CASHIER SUBMISSION TEMPLATE

DATE	CASHIER NAME	CASH REMITTED	TRANSFER	POS	TOTAL
2/10/2002	DAVID	50000	120000	250000	420000
	MARY	18000	150000	318000	486000

This book is used to record cash POS, and transfer collected from cashiers, it's advisable to instruct chief cashiers to mop out this collectible within short time interval, to reduce cash volume with cashiers.

Cashier remission book: This book is given to cashiers to record their POS, cash, and transfer collected from them by the chief cashier. The format of this book is exactly like the cashier submission book, the only difference is that chief cashier book records different cashier on the same book. But the cashier remission book has records for one cashier a day, and a signature column to confirm receiving the collectibles.

CASHIER REMISSION TEMPLATE

DATE	CASHIER NAME	CASH REMITTED	TRANSFER	POS	TOTAL	SIGN
2/10/2002	DAVID	50000	120000	250000	420000	QX
		300000	45000	340000	685000	QX

Daily Sales Analysis: This book records cash flow transfer, and POS and how cash remitted are used in the store. At beginning of a fiscal period an opening cash is created, which the cash balance is added to the cash remitted for the day, expenses and purchases for the day are deducted from the total available cash to get the closing cash balance. See the image below for a template of a daily sales log book.

DAILY SALES ANALYSIS TEMPLATE

DATE	OPENING CASH	CASH REMITTED	TRANSFER/POS	TOTAL		BANK PAYME	PURCHASE/EXPENSES	CLOSING CASH
2/10/2002	1200000	350000	780000	1215000		200000	COCA COLA 850000	345,000
			TRANSFER				REKITT BENKISER 150000	
			85000				PAYMENT FOR FUEL 5000	
							TOTAL: 1,005,000	
3/10/2002								

Payment book

See the image below for a payment book

PAYMENT BOOK

INVOICE NAME	INVOICE NO	DEPT	QUANTITY	AMOUNT	PHONE NO.	SIGN
		16/5/2002				
REKITT BENKISER	9045	TOILETRIES	200PCKS	850,000	09065XX8745	QX
COCA-COLA	4567	DRINKS	650PACKS	1,100,000	0804565XX56	QX
				1,950,000		
		17/5/2022				

See the image below for a supply register

SUPPLIER REGISTER

INVOICE NAME	INVOICE NO	DEPT	QUANTITY	AMOUNT	PHONE NO.	SIGN
		16/5/2002				
REKITT BENKISER	9045	TOILETRIES	200PCKS	850,000	09065XX8745	QX
COCA-COLA	4567	DRINKS	650PACKS	1,100,000	0804565XX56	QX
				1,950,000		
		17/5/2022				

Chart of Accounts Developing a well-structured chart of accounts is crucial for organizing financial data. A chart account is a categorization system that assigns a unique code to different financial activities. Common categories include sales, cost of goods sold (COGS), operating expenses, and taxes. This framework facilitates easier tracking and reporting of financial information.

Cost of Goods Sold (COGS) COGS represents the direct costs associated with producing or purchasing the store's overall financial health.

Tax Compliance adhering to tax regulations is crucial for avoiding legal issues. Proper accounting ensures accurate calculation and timely payment of taxes, including sales tax, income tax, and payroll tax. Maintaining organized records simplifies the tax filing process.

Accounting Software and Technology Many grocery stores rely on accounting software to streamline financial management processes. These tools automate tasks like data entry, report generation, and reconciliation, saving time and reducing the risk of errors.

In the dynamic world of grocery retail, effective accounting practices are indispensable for achieving financial success. Proper record-keeping, inventory management, expense tracking, and the use of technology contribute to the smooth functioning of a grocery store. By embracing these practices, store owners can make informed decisions, maximize profitability, and ensure long-term sustainability.

Accounting positions and hiring standards for professionals

Any business's ability to succeed strongly depends on the integrity and accuracy of its financial data. For financial operations to run smoothly and regulations to be followed, qualified accounting professionals must be employed. Finding the best people with the required abilities, knowledge, and qualities is a crucial procedure that needs considerable thought. In this post, we'll look at the essential requirements for hiring qualified accountants who can improve the financial stability of your company.

1. Academic credentials and professional credentials

The educational background and professional certifications of prospective accounting staff are one of the basic standards for choosing qualified candidates. Candidates with pertinent degrees, like a Bachelor's or Master's in Accounting or Finance, exhibit a strong foundation in principles.

Additionally, certifications like Certified Public Accountant (CPA), Chartered Accountant (CA), or Certified Management Accountant (CMA) indicate a high level of expertise and commitment to the field.

2. Technical Proficiency

Accounting role requires a strong grasp of financial software and tools. Candidates should be proficient in using accounting software such as QuickBooks, SAP, or Oracle, depending on your organization's preferences. Proficiency in spreadsheet applications like Microsoft Excel is also a must, as these tools are essential for data analysis, financial modelling, and reporting.

3. Attention to Detail

Accounting is a precise discipline that necessitates a high level of precision. Accounting professionals should have a sharp eye for detail and an unshakable devotion to correctness. Financial record errors can result in costly errors, legal ramifications, and damage to the company's reputation.

4. Analytical Capabilities

Accounting workers must be analytical in understanding financial data, spot trends, and make sound recommendations. They can provide vital insights into strategic decision-making within the organization by analyzing financial data, budgets, and predictions.

5. Moral Integrity

Accounting professionals deal with sensitive financial information and are held to the highest ethical standards. Integrity is essential in this sector because any wrongdoing or unethical behavior can lead to financial fraud, legal problems, and loss of trust from stakeholders.

6. Communication Skills

Accounting personnel must be able to communicate effectively in collaboration with colleagues from other departments, explain difficult financial ideas to non-financial stakeholders, and generate accurate and comprehensible reportsts. Strong written and spoken communication abilities promote the exchange of information.

7. Organization and time management

Accounting entails managing a variety of activities, deadlines, and responsibilities. Accounting professionals should be able to prioritize projects, manage their time effectively, and regularly fulfil deadlines. They can maintain track of various financial records and transactions with the help of effective organizational skills.

8. Adaptability and Lifelong Learning

Accounting is a constantly changing field, with changes in legislation, norms, and technologies. Continuous learning allows competent accounting professionals to stay current with industry developments, legislation, and best practices. Adaptability to new software, techniques, and accounting standards changes is an essential traits.

Selecting competent accounting employees is a crucial process that demands careful consideration of multiple criteria. Beyond technical skills, educational qualifications, and certifications, candidates should possess attributes such as attention to detail, analytical skills, ethical integrity, effective communication, and time management abilities. A successful accounting team contributes significantly to the financial health and growth of an organization, making the selection of competent employees a pivotal decision. By adhering to these criteria, businesses can ensure they have the right talent in place to manage their financial operations effectively.

In the next chapter, "Marketing and Advertising," we will delve deeper into developing a comprehensive marketing strategy, utilizing traditional and digital marketing channels, creating a brand identity, and fostering community engagement to attract and retain customers.

MARKETING AND ADVERTISING

Effective marketing and promotion are critical in attracting customers, developing brand identification, and promoting your grocery store's success. We will look at four major areas to focus on in this chapter: constructing a thorough marketing plan, utilizing traditional and digital marketing channels, creating a brand identity and promoting store loyalty, gigs with the local community, and forming collaborations. By using these tactics, you can increase your sales by incorporating the following elements:

Sales promotion for the first introduction: This method should be used by each new store that wants to generate a lot of money and gain a lot of attention. When the business first opens, there will be a promotion in which the first 1000 customers to buy will receive a set percentage discount. This can be broadcast on television, social media, and other platforms. It depends on your budget and the target customers that you intend to reach. Target Market Analysis: Identify your target audience based on demographics, preferences, and shopping behaviors. Tailor your meeting messages and channels accordingly.

Unique Selling Proposition (USP): Determine whether you receive distinctive features and a value proposition that distinguishes you from competition. To attract customers, highlight these in your marketing.

Marketing Objectives: For your marketing activities, set specified, measurable, achievable, relevant, and time-bound (SMART) goals. Increased foot traffic, best exclusively online sales, or promoting new product launches are among examples.

Marketing Budget: Set aside a reasonable amount of money for marketing initiatives, taking into account channels, campaigns, and continuing promotions. Keep track of your expenditures and make adjustments based on the return on investment (ROI).

Making use of traditional and digital marketing channels:

Use a combination of traditional and digital marketing platforms to reach a larger audience. Consider the following alternatives:

Traditional Channels: Advertise special discounts, sales, or events in print media such as local newspapers, periodicals, and community newsletters. Consider radio and direct mail marketing that target certain neighborhoods.

Leverage the power of the internet and digital platforms through digital channels. Create a professional website that highlights your store's items, gives store information, and, if applicable, facilitates online ordering. Use search engine optimization (SEO) tactics to increase the visibility of your website on search engines. Engage clients on social media sites, communicate updates, and perform targeted ad campaigns. Investigate email marketing as a means of reaching out to your customer base with personalized offers and newsletters.

Developing a brand identity and encouraging customer loyalty:

A strong brand identity fosters customer trust and loyalty. Consider the following approaches:

Choose a memorable store name and create a visually appealing logo that expresses your store's beliefs and resonates with your target audience.

Maintain consistent branding throughout all marketing assets, such as signage, packaging, and internet platforms. To enhance your brand identity, use consistent colors, fonts, and messaging.

Create a beautiful and engaging store environment that is consistent with your brand image. To improve the shopping experience, pay attention to store layout, lighting, and music.

Implement a loyalty programme that rewards customers for their continuing support. To encourage repeat purchases and foster customer loyalty, provide incentives such as unique discounts, personalized offers, or freebies.

Engaging with the local community and establishing partnerships:

Community involvement can assist your store in becoming a trusted and vital member of the local community. Consider the following strategies:

Participate in community events, fund community initiatives, or offer workshops or cooking classes about grocery shopping or healthy eating. This highlights your store's involvement and creates positive customer relationships.

Collaborations: Work with local businesses, farms, or food producers to offer unique items or special promotions. Collaboration with community organizations or charities for fundraising efforts can also help your store's reputation.

Local Marketing: Target your marketing efforts on the community where you live. Promote seasonal produce from regional farms, or fund local sports teams or school events. To reach a larger audience, collaborate with local influencers or bloggers. By developing a comprehensive marketing strategy, utilizing various channels, creating a strong brand identity, and engaging with the local community, you can effectively market your grocery store and cultivate loyal customers.

In the next chapter, "Creating a Positive Shopping Experience," we will discuss the importance of store aesthetics and ambiance, ensuring cleanliness and organization, providing amenities and convenient services, and fostering excellent customer service to create a welcoming and enjoyable shopping experience for your customers.

CREATING A POSITIVE SHOPPING EXPERIENCE

The shopping experience is critical in recruiting and retaining customers in your supermarket. This chapter will go over four major aspects to consider: store aesthetics and ambiance, cleanliness and organization, amenities and handy services, and developing exceptional customer service and personalized experiences. You can create a pleasant and engaging workplace that increases customer satisfaction and loyalty by prioritizing these characteristics.

Store aesthetics and ambiance: Your store's visual attractiveness and environment have a significant impact on the overall shopping experience. Take a look at the following:

Store Design: Create a logical and simple layout that directs clients through different sections and ensures they can easily access things. Organize shelves and displays in a logical manner, with clear signage for simple identification.

Optimize lighting to produce a bright and welcoming atmosphere. To improve product visibility and accent specific sections or displays, use a combination of natural and artificial lighting.

Visual merchandising is the creation of aesthetically appealing displays that exhibit things in an appealing manner. To attract clients' attention, use smart color palettes, seasonal decorations, and eye-catching signage.

Music and scent: Choose background music that complements the mood of your store and its target demographic. Consider integrating delicate scents associated with fresh fruit or bakery items that elicit positive sentiments.

Maintaining cleanliness and organization: A clean and organized store is essential for consumer happiness and safety. Consider the following methods: Regular Cleaning: Establish a strict cleaning schedule for all areas of the store, including aisles, shelves, restrooms, and storage areas. Pay attention to high-traffic areas and frequently touched surfaces.

Sanitation and Food Safety: To ensure food safety, adhere to proper cleanliness practices. Inspect and monitor perishable materials on a regular basis, and follow proper storage and handling procedures.

Product Freshness: Check product expiration dates on a

regular basis and remove any expired or damaged items from the shelf as soon as possible. Refrigerate perishable foods to maintain their quality and freshness.

Use clear and informative signs to orient clients and help them locate different product categories, clearance goods, or special deals across the store.

Providing facilities and useful services:

Offering extra facilities and convenient services can improve the entire shopping experience and help your store stand out. Take a look at the following:

Baskets and shopping carts: Make sure there are enough shopping carts and baskets for customers to utilize. Inspect and maintain them on a regular basis for functionality and cleanliness.

Checkout Efficiency: Make the checkout process more efficient by providing enough workers and checkout lanes to reduce wait times. Consider offering self-checkout choices to customers who desire a faster checkout experience.

Rest Area and Seating: Designate a rest area with seating for guests who may require a break throughout their shopping trip. Provide comfortable seating and possibly a beverage station for added convenience.

Online Ordering and Delivery: Allow clients who prefer to shop from home to place orders online. To meet their demands, provide delivery or curbside collection services.

Improving customer service and providing personalized experiences:

Outstanding customer service distinguishes your grocery business from the competition. Consider the following approaches:

Staff that is well-trained: Train your employees to be kind and informed when assisting consumers. Encourage them to connect with you in a polite manner, to provide product recommendations, and provide prompt support when needed.

Personalized Recommendations: Teach employees about their consumers' requirements and preferences. Encourage them to make personalized recommendations based on dietary needs, recipes, or product enquiries.

Implement a loyalty programme that rewards customers for their continuing support. Show your thanks by providing personalized discounts, customized deals, or unique advantages to show appreciation for their loyalty.

Encourage your customers to submit feedback and suggestions. Actively listen to their concerns, respond to any difficulties as soon as possible, and consider integrating their suggestions to improve the entire shopping experience.

You can create a great and memorable shopping experience that increases customer loyalty and word-of-mouth recommendations by prioritizing store aesthetics, cleanliness, convenience, and exceptional customer service.

In the following chapter, "Conclusion," we will summarize the important themes mentioned throughout the eBook and offer last suggestions and reminders to aspiring grocery shop entrepreneurs.

CONCLUSION

You've made it to the final chapter of "How to Run a Successful Grocery Store." Throughout this eBook, we've looked at the key procedures and factors involved in starting and running a successful grocery shop. Let's take time to review the main points mentioned, offer encouragement to aspiring grocery store entrepreneurs, and offer some final success suggestions and reminders.

1. Review of main themes covered in the eBook:

• Conduct extensive market research and planning in order to understand your target market, competitors, and the viability of your grocery store operation.

• Select the best location by taking into account aspects including population density, demography, proximity to residential areas and transit, as well as zoning and regulatory needs.

• Create a visually appealing and functional store layout that maximizes product placement, aisle organization, and checkout systems.

   Establish reliable supplier relationships and prioritize product quality, freshness, and variety.

• Determine staffing needs, recruit competent employees, provide training in customer service and product knowledge, and implement performance evaluation and incentives.•

Embrace technology and implement systems like a point-of-sale (POS) system, inventory management software, and effective accounting and bookkeeping systems.

• Create a comprehensive marketing strategy that combines traditional and digital media to advertise your grocery shop, establish a brand identity, and engage with the local community.

• Focus on store aesthetics, cleanliness, convenience, and good customer service to create a positive shopping experience.

2. Motivation and encouragement for potential grocery shop owners: Setting up a grocery business involves a lot of passion, dedication, and perseverance. Keep in mind that you've chosen an industry that delivers a valuable service to the community and has the potential for long-term success. Maintain a positive perspective throughout the process, stay focused on your vision, and welcome challenges as learning opportunities. Your hard work and dedication will pave the road for a rewarding and fulfilling entrepreneurial adventure.

3. Final tips and reminders for success in setting up a grocery store:

• Continuously monitor and adapt to changing market trends, customer preferences, and industry advancements.

• Foster strong relationships with customers, suppliers, and the local community through open communication, responsiveness, and genuine care.

• Stay updated on industry regulations, food safety standards, and compliance requirements to ensure smooth operations

• Prioritize continual staff training and development to improve their skills and expertise, resulting in better customer service. • Review and analyze financial performance on a regular basis, change pricing strategies, and optimize inventory management to maximize profitability.

• Look for chances for distinction and innovation, such as unique product offerings, exclusive alliances, or personalized consumer experiences.

Remember that the success of your grocery shop is dependent on careful planning, excellent execution, and a dedication to ongoing improvement. Accept the obstacles, enjoy the rewards, and build a grocery shop that becomes a beloved part of the community.

Best wishes on your journey of opening and operating a

successful grocery store. You may thrive in this dynamic and profitable profession if you have the correct strategies, perseverance, and desire.

The following product you need to have in a supermarket considering your location, is in Lagos. You must buy small quantities to know the products that are your high-selling products and increase the quantity.

GROCERY STORE SECRETS

There are some essential activities that a grocery stores must engage in to improve sales which working for many mega stores. In this segment I will highlight some necessary strategies works currently for both sales and inventory security.

1. Restocking: when procurement officer buying products for the store advise them to buy new products. A store that has new product is always know to a store that sells everything. Encourage floor employee to take note of any product that a customer request for that is not in stock. Ensure you never run out of stock, have restock level for every products. Because when you go out of stock of some products often, you will give your customers the opportunity to buy from competitor which might discourage them from patronizing your store when they buy at a cheaper rate.

2. Price: Don't joke with your price margin as a new entrant store the price you enter the market with, will determine he volume of sales turnover that you will receive. Make your daily need products have a reasonable mark up to attract customers while the other section can be your profit machine. The turnover on the daily use products will reflect on the other sections that has high profit margin.

3. Survey: In grocery store it's imperative to check the price competitors are currently selling to beat their price with little token for massive sales.

4. Employee treatment: Provide a comfortable condition for employees that match their status of work. Considering this requires a thorough questioning while employing them to know your organization can provide a perfect working condition for employees. Eatable in shop by employees should be regulated and controlled by placing a law of submitting invoice to the store manager for every products purchased in the shop to have a close watch items that are paid for before eating.

5. Avoid long wait on the cash point, ensure you have enough cashier that can control your pick for swift check out.

The products listed below can be used as a start list for your grocery store in Nigeria. For those reading this training manual from other countries you can look through the list to get hunch on some products that are needed in your store.

PROVISION	Café d vita
	Nestle coffee mate big and small
Kelloggs cornflakes all sizes	Nesquick big size
Kelloggs frosties big and small	Peak 123 tin and refill
Fruit n fibre big and small	Peak 456 tin and refill
Frosted flakes	Cowbell tin and refill 400g
Raisin bran	Loya tin and refill 400g'
Bran flakes	Marvel milk big and small
Honey bunches	Peak 0-12months tin and refill
Fruit loops	Nido tin all sizes
K special	Complan
Frosties big and small	Oluji cocoa powder tin and refill
Rice Krispies	Milo tin and refill 400g
Infinity cornflakes big and small	Milo tin and refill 800g
Nasco cornflakes	Milo 2kg tin
Imported Kellogg's coco pops big and small	Milo refill 1.8kg
Nigeria coco pops	Ovaltine tin and refill all sizes
Nigeria cornflakes	Bourvita jar big and small
	Bournvita refill
	Peak tin 900g

Crown Field fruit and fiber	Peak refill 800g
Millville cornflakes	Cowbell refill 800g
Millville fruit and fibre	Dano cool cow refill 360g, 800g, 2kg
Nasco cornflakes sarchet	Dano refill 360g, 800g, 2kg
Cocopos sarchet	Dano cool cow tin 900g
Moon and star sarchet	Dano tin 900g
Moon and star 400g	Dano slim refill big and small
Crownfield granola	Nan 1, 2, and 3 tin
Harvest morn granola	Aptamil 1, 2, 3, and 4
Harvest morn cornflakes	Enfamil baby
Weetabix minis	Glucose d
Weetabix assorted variants	Friso gold rice and wheat
Nescafe gold blend decaff	Sma gold big and small 1,2, and 3.
Nescafe gold blend all size	Miksi refill
Nescafe tin	Bournvita refill
Nescafe 3 in 1 coffee sachet	Cheer up oats
Nescafe sticks	Lecker oats
Davidoff coffee	Tropical sun oat big and small
Medium roast coffee	Cadbury 3 in 1 refill and sarchet
Bellarom coffee	Cerelac big and small
	Nutriben breakfast
Peak milk sarchet	

Dano milk sarchet	Nutribom assorted variants
Dano cool cow milk sarchet	
Three crown milk sarchet	Blueband 450g spread and original
Peak milk sarchet	
Milo sarchet	Blueband 900g spread and original
Bournvita sarchet	Golden penny spread all sizes
Loya milk sarchet	Kings spread
My boy eldorin milk tikn	Summer field spread
Quaker oat old fashion and quick cook	Moi spread big and small
Milleville quaker oat old fashion and quick cook	Remia-vital-spread
	Mamador-spread
	Just-magarine
Campville rolled oats	Heinz-mayonaise-big&small
Honeyville rolled oad	Bama mayonnaise small, medium, & big
Fashion club oat jar	Jago mayonnaise big and medium
Quaker oat refill	Wippy mayonnaise big, small and medium
Quaker oat sarchet	
Quaker oat tin	Skippy all variants big and small
Peak milk tin 2500g	Nutzy spread all variants
Nido milk 2500g	Vigo choco spread
Peak Nigeria liquid tin	Kirkland hazelnut spread
Peak holand liquid tin	

Three crown milk tin

Dogan sugar cubes

Dogan brown sugar

Nice brown sugar granulated and cubes

St Louis sugar cubes

Golden penny sugar cubes

Golden penny granulated sugar

Bolero big and small

Birds custard big and small

Golds custard big and small

Lady b custard big and small

Checkers vanilla 2kg 400g

Checkers 3in 1.5kg and 400g

Checkers banana big and small

Family custard 1.5kg

Nutriben cereal

Frontera all variants

Lamotte parrot all variants

Four cousin all variants

WINES

Escudo rojo wine

Nederburg all variants wine

Drosdyoff big and small

B&g cuvee special

Bastardo wine

Sierra wine

Carlo rossi all variants

Dorado

Baron romero

Baron devalls

Two oceans all variants

Cape more

Blossom hill

Casto negro

Agor wine

Classic acolerex

Chealsea gin big, medium and

De clan all variants	small
Eco falls wine	Squadron run
Castillo de rossi	Vegas brandy
6 sens wines	St remy vsop, and xo.
Eva wine	Hennessy vs, vsop, xo. remy martin
Pure heaven wine	Martell vs
Welchs white and red	Martell blue swift
Martinellis big and small	Jameson black barrel
Shloer all variants	Red label big and small
Chamdor white and red	Black label
Veleta wine	Johnie walker double black
J&w wine	Gold label
J&w sparkling	Sky vodka
Valentine wine	Flirt vodka
Best cream small and big	Grand master vodka
Best whisky small and big	Absolut vodka
Best gin small and big	Smirnoff vodka
Lords gin big and small	Matrix vodka
Jameson big and small	Barcadi vodka
Campari all sizes	Gleffiddich 12yrs, 15yrs, 18yrs, and 21yrs
Mc dowels all sizes	Macallan 12yrs, 15yrs, and 18yrs
Magic moment all sizes	

Ceres red and white grape bottle	moet brut and rose
Baileys cream big and small	singleton whisky 12yrs and 15yrs
Baileys delight	Jack Daniels whisky and honey
Bardinet grenadine	Gentle man jack
Andre rose and brut	Jagermeiter big and small
Night train	Kuemerling all sizes
Baccus wine	Seaman all sizes
Castillo de liria	Eagle schnapps
Angustural bitters	Olmeca tequila all variants
Joven capel	Status vodka
Finca challion	Crystal palace vodka
Mogen david	Grants whisky
Lambrusco wine	
Orijin bitters big and small	
Alomo bitters	
Action bitters 750ml,375, and 200ml	
	Goldberg can
LIQUID MILK	Smirnoff red and black can
Dano all variants 1lt	Heineken can
Peak all variants1lt	Budweiser can
Emborg all variants 1lt	Maltina can and pet all variants

Blue diamond milk	Amstel can and plastic
Kirkland milk	Amstel ultra can
Alpro milk	Malta guiness can plastic
Vitamilk soya milk 1lt	Snapple
Hollandika milk 1lt	Ceres orange, pineapple, red grape,& apple
Rita milk all variants	Ceres red and white can
Vita milk bottle	
Kirkland non-dairy milk	Stute cranberry, mango, orange, tropical.
Ensure milk	Greek yoghurt
Ensure plus	Parfait
Pedia sure milk	Hollandia yoghurt plain and strawberry
Glucernar milk	Chivita active all sizes
	Chi ice tea all sizes
	Chi happy hour all sizes
	Chi exotic all sizes
DRINKS	Farm pride juices
coke pet 50cl,35cl and can	Farmfeast yoghurt
fanta pet 50cl,35cl and can	Pure heaven can
sprite pet 50cl,35cl and can	Black bullet and blue bullet
5 berry blast 78cl	Power horse
5 alive pulpy orange 30cl and 85cl	Fearless

Schweppes can	Getorade juice
Eva water 75cl and 150cl	Red bull can
Predator	Apple and eve pet and pack
Monster can	Ribena gold 850ml and 1.5lt
Pepsi pet and can	Ribena red cover
Aquafina water all sizes	Realemon juice
Teem lemon and soda	Trs lemon juice
Mirinda pet	Chefs lime juice
Welchs pet	Trs lime juice
Ocean spray pet big and small	Okf smoothie
Canada dry	Don simon 1lt
Ginger beer	Don simon can
Old Jamaica	Ribena 1lt pack
Fayrouz can	
Stout can	
	Lemon tea
	Legend tea
COOKING OIL	True slim tea
Wesson canola & vegetable 4.9lt	Tommy flat tea
	Ulcer tea
Laser oil pomace 500ml, 1lt, and 4l	La botti tea
Laser oil extra virgin 500ml,	Bigelow tea

1lt	New life tea
Laser oil 5lt	Qualitea tea
Kings 1lt, 2lt, 3lt, 5lt	Lipton decaff tea
Mamador oil 900ml, 1.5lt, 2.5lt, and 3.5ml	Lipton black tea
Laziz oil 1lt, 3lt and 5lt	
Okomu 4lt, and 2lt	
Power oil 7.5cl, 1.5cl, 2.6lt, 4.5lt	
Saffola oil 5lt	
Olivari avocado oil	CONDIMENTS
Goya oil all sizes	Nutella all sizes
Wesson oil 1lt	Nutzzy all sizes
Cassa de campo oil 5lt	Skippy all sizes
leisure oil	Nussa all sizes
basso oil	Light Soy sauce big and small
grand oil all sizes	Dark soy sauce
	Sesame oil big and small
	Amoy sauce big and small
	Heinz yellow mustard
	Trs dicipated coconut
TEA	Oyster sauce big and small
3 Ballerina tea	Hp bbq sauce all variants
Twining tea by chamomile	

California tea	Amoy shawarma sauce
Ahmed tea	Wish bone thousand island
Twining tea assorted variants	California fresh style sauce
Edmark tea all variants	Latyf Vinegar
Alliance tea cappuccino, sugar free	Heinz vinegar
	Bragg vinegar big and small
Red yeast tea	Fally White vinegar
Café 57 tea	Chilli pepper big and small
Tetley tea	Spice supreme spices all variants small
Lipton tea	
Top tea	Spice supreme big curry and thyme
Top tea lemon	
Ginger tea	
Bbq sauce	Exeter Argentina corned beef
Goya adobo all variant and sizes	Farrows big and small
	Coconut milk maling and other variants
Lion curry and thyme	
Tropical sun seasoning all variants	Emma coconut powder
	Saxon everything mix spice
Ducros curry and thyme	Dinor mushroom and other variants
Banga spices	
Remia salad cream	Blue pearl red kidney beans
Heinz Italian salad dressing	Blue pearl macedone mixed veg
	Princess hot dog

Remia thousand island	Ham
Remia frech salad cream	Sunripe peas
Laziz salad cream	Titus, milo, napa, geisha sardines and other brands
Ktc castor oil	Princess sardine, and tuna fish
Kirkland coconut oil	John west tuna fish and other new tune fish
Honey product in bottle	
Laser honey	Hershey syrup
Rose honey	Foster clark flavours all variants
New bottle honey	Hungry jack pancake mix
Real honey	Hungry jack syrup
Guert jam all variants	Aunty jemaima syrup
Stute jam all variants	Arm and hammer baking soda
Mr chef salt 250g, 500g, and 1kg	Joe baking soda big and small
Dangote salt 250g, 500g, and 1kg	Stk royal yeast
	Susan corn flour
Pink himakilayan salt	Mc dougalls flour big and small
Best one Table salt and other new brands	Mixed dried fruit
	Coconut flakes
Saxa salt	Packed eggs
Costa fine and coarse salt	Couscous sipa
Bay leaves	Blue pearl prawns
Tiger seasoning all sizes and variants	Golden penny couscous

Batts ketchup	Double t ofada rice
Heinz ketchup all sizes	Brown beans
Bramwells tomato ketchep	White beans
Alfa ketchup	Golden penny spaghetti
Frolic ketchup	Golden penny macaroni
American vinegar	Golden penny twist
Laziz tomato ketchup	Crown spaghetti
Napa corned beef big and small	Barilla spaghetti and macaroni
Heinz beanz big and small	Bonita spaghetti
Other brands baked beanz	SNACKS AND BISCUITS
Sunripe sweet corn big and small	Pringles all sizes and variants
Green giant sweet corn big and small	Tropical sun peanuts all sizes and variants
Exeter corned brazil beef big and small	Executive cashew all variants and sizes
Simply spaghetti	Kohkoa peanut
Ayoola poundo 0.9kg, 2.2kg and 4.5kg	Burger peanut tin and sarchet
	Trs almond nut all sizes
Ayoola plantain 0.9kg, 2.2kg and 4.5kg	Yale cabin
Ayoola yam flour 0.9kg, 2.2kg and 4.5kg	Oxford cabin
	Nutro malted milk biscuit
Ayoola Beans flour 2.2kg	Frya soda cracker by 12

Ayoola beans 0.9kg, 2.2kg and 4.5kg	Jacobs water
Ola ola poundo yam 0.9kg, 2.2kg and 4.5kg	Soda cracker by 10 and by 24
	Jacobs cracker big and small
Elkris oat meal	Mc vities Rich tea big and small
Oatala oat meal	Pure bliss all variants
Garri brands	Super 2 biscuit
Golden penny semovita 900g, 2kg, 5kg, 10kg	Fadaella oat biscuit
	Tuc cracker
Honeywell 900g, 2kg, 5kg, and 10kg	Ritz crackers
Mama gold 2kg and 5kg	Tower gate cookies all variants
Knorr chicken, and cubes	Merba chocolate cookies
Star cubes and chicken	New Yorkers cookies
Rayco maggi	Tower gate rich tea
Star maggi packets	Sky flakes crackers
Star maggi chicken pot big and small	Desmond crackers
	Maryland cookies all variants
Par excellence rice all sizes	Belloxy cracker all sizes
Aeroplace rice all sizes	Diabetamil cookies
Maharani rice 5kg and 1kg	Gerber baby biscuit
Golden sella rice basmatic all variants all sizes	Tower gate malted milk
	Digestive 400g, 250g and 40g
Tilda basmatic rice 5kg and 10kg	Elkes malted milk

Trs basmatic rice	Hobnobs all sizes
Gino perfume rice 500g and 5kg	Tower gate short bread
Laila brown rice 2kg and 5kg	Mc vities shortbread all sizes
Lalquila brown rice 5kg	Tom tom
Indomie all sizes and variants	Vick blue and lemon
Gino spaghetti	Buttermint
Crown spaghetti and macaroni	Kopiko sweet
Asda spaghetti and macaroni	Pin pop sweet
Dangote spaghetti	Chupa chups gum
Power pasta	Chupa chupe sweet
Honeywell pasta	Maltesers all sizes
Nutric pack	Belmont digestive
Mustard seed	Belmont oaties
Chia seed	Nutria snax
	Mc vities ginger nut
	Royal ginger nut
	Digestive oaties
	Splash sweet
Twix chocolate	Ogl shortbread
Pectol gum	Borders biscuit
Mentos gum	Famous amos
Orbit gum all variants	Oreos by 30

Alpenlebe	Oreos by 12
Haribo golds bears	Oreos by 10
Haribo marshmello	Smarties all sizes
	M&m cookies
	Nature valley oat
Red disposable cup	Kemps crackers
White disposable cup	Coaster crackers
Disposable plate	Beloxxy minis
Takeaway plate big and small	Ferroro rocher all sizes
Table pans big and small	Kerk cream crackers
Disposable plate	Mcvities biscuits dark chocolate
Toothpick variety	Mc vities chocolate
Tooth pick varies	Fox chunkies all variants
Matches	Danish cookies
Gas lighter and small lighter	Hellama spectacular
Cling film big and small variety	Carl cracker
Foil paper big and small variety	
Baking paper	M&m chocolates
Ziploc all sizes	Toblerone chocolate dark and white
Disposable white spoon and fork	Diary milk all sizes and variants
Disposable color spoon and	

fork	Bon o bon chocolate
Spatula stick	Eclairs all sizes
bowl plate	Snickers chocolate
asun plate big and small	Mars chocolate
stainless spoon and fork	Bounty chocolate
	Dettol disinfectant all sizes
	Septol disinfectant all sizes
	Premier disinfect 500ml mad 1lt
	Temosol disinfectant all sizes
	Savlon disinfectant all sizes
	St ives tablet soap
	Kbrothers soap big and small bbclearsoap all variants gluta c soap
	Fair child soap
TOILETRIES	Extract soap Nigeria
Kirkland kitchen towel	Extract soap foreign
Bounty kitchen towel	F&w so white
Rose plus towel	Fair and white exclusive vit c and normal
Carla towel	

Rose select towel	Bio oil soap
Andrex tissue	Extract big
Kirkland bath tissue	4 in 1 koji soap all variants
Member mark bath tissue	Rapid-white-soap
Rose bell tissue box	Pure-skin-soap
Vicki tissue box	So-fruity-soap
Kleenex tissue box	half cast all variants
Rose Carla tissue	Gluthathion soap
Rose belle tissue	Hawaii soap all variants
Rose plus tissue	Veet gold soap
Paloma tissue	Olay soap
Swantex tissue serviet	Rhome soap
Rose belle serviet	Valderma soap
Tampax all variants	Wright soap
Drylove pads	Half cast soap pink and black
Kedi pads	Asantee soap big and small all variants
Longrigh pads and liners	Clinic care gold soap
Always pads single and double pink and blue	Gold skin soap green and yellow pack
Always by 90	Peneca moringa and carrot soap
Always by 120	Eden soap all variants
Always platinium single and double	Idole soap all variants

Always cotton pads	Smooth as silk big and small
Molped all variants	Tcp soap
Candle	Tetmosol big and small
Ghana must go	Cusson baby soap
Slippers	Johnson Baby soap
Bin bag yellow and green label	Eva baby soap booth baby soap
Slippers	Pears transparent all variants
Shoe Spray polish	Eva soap all variants
Padlocks mix	Caro white soap
Shoe foam	Pure white soap
Shoe oil	Carotone soap
Shoe brush	White secret soap
Kiwi polish big and small	Dove soap all variants
Diplomat all variants	Nano extra white soap
Oral b toothbrush all variant	Kojic acid soap
Colgate tooth brush all variants	Axi kojic acid soap
Wisdom brush	Kojic acid naked
Sensodyne tooth brush	Dr rashel soap
Listerine reach tooth brush	Ct plus soap
Molfix jumbo all sizes	Irish spring soap nig and foreign
Molfix eco all sizes	Caro white soap
	Neutrogena soap

Molfix mini all sizes	Jenifer lopez secret all variants
Huggies Nigeria all sizes	Safeguard all variants and size
Molfix pant all sizes	Dettol soap all variants and sizes
Hugies imported all sizes	
Kirkland wipes	
Hugies wipes all variants	Wind block big and small all variants
Abc wipes	Candle air freshner
Molfix wipes	Automatic airfreshner
Angel wipes	Airwick refill
Johnsons wipes	California scents
Clorox wipes	Exotic scents can
Virony wipes	Abro scent can
Pretty intimate pntyliners	Airwick drummer
Kotex pantiliner and pads	Sunshine block and gel
	Wind gel big and small
	Glade gel
	Airwick Diffuser
	Glade diffuser
	Lu blue
Xoc tooth paste	Harpic hanger
Kedi paste	Swiss airfreshner
Dabur herbal paste all	

variants	Ambi pur case and refill
Longrich paste	Gbc refill
Close up paste all variants	Car dashboard air freshner
Close up red small	Hapic all variants big and small
Papsodent all variants	Gbc exol big and small
Colgate tooth paste all variants	Harpic green, black, white, and pink
One family paste	Jik all sizes
Euthymol	Hypo toilet cleaner big, small and sarchet
Macleean paste all variants and sizes	Parazone bleach
Crest paste uk	Domestos bleach
Crest paste usa	Tiscol 4lt
Sensodyne all variants	Deep clean 4lt and 1lt
Oral b all varaints and sizes	Comfort all sizes and variants
Renew cold water starch	Persil liquid
Hot water starch	Persil in cup
Renew spray starch	Omo in box
Canoe soap all variants and sizes	Tide automatic
Sunlight soap all variats	Persil all sizes and variants
Duduosun	Lysol spray
Imperial leather soap all sizes	Pledge
	Mr sheen

Joy soap all sizes	Wisdom mouth wash
F29 soap	Colgate mouth wash
Hypo sarchet	Aquafresh mouth wash
2sure soap	Listerine mouth wash all sizes
Septol soap	Odour vanish
Oki soap	Ambi pur airfreshner
Waw soap big and small	English breeze spray
Premier soap by 30	5in1 spray airfreshner
Tura supreme soap	Swiss airfreshner all sizes
Viva soap all variants	Easy on spray starch
Premier cool big and small	Faultless spray starch and other new brands
Ivory soap all variants	Persil powder all sizes and variants
Nature fresh soap	Morning fresh all sizes and variants
Nigertol disinfectant	Mama lemon big and small and other dish wash l;iquids
Hypo bleach all sizes and variants	Ariel detergent all sizes
Lb car wash all sizes	Omo detergents all sizes
Lb fabric 4lt, 2lt, and 1lt	Sunlight detergent all sizes
Lb bath and toilet cleaner	Good mama detergent all sizes
Windolene	Klin all sizes
Astonish kitchen cleaner, bathroom, floor, leather cleaner, and stainless shower	Viva detergent all sizes

Other types of windolene	Canoe detergent
Limpo clean	Zip detergent
Cif cleaner	
Cif cream	
Vim scouring powder	
Other variants scouring powder	HOUSE HOLDS
	Kenwood Blender
Palmolive hand wash	Philip blender
Astonish hand wash	Oris blender
Dettol hand wash	Smart home blender
Carex hand wash	Electric kettle different variants
Sparkle hand wash	Electric jug different variant
English breeze hand wash	Pressing iron different variants
	Microwaves different variants
TOYS	Yam poundo
Basket ball	Industrial blender
Chess	Hair dryer
Scrabble	Airfryer different variants
Ludo	Deep fryer
Monopoly	Oven
Draft	Mixer
Building blocks	Lint roller

Teddy bear	Dehumidifier
Female doll	Hubbner 6pcs plate and other brands
Character doll	Pramid hot plate
Male doll	Sandwich toaster
Gear peacock	Cook set 8pcs and 6ps
Memory ,match	Mug
Bubble gun	Dish rack plastic and wooden
Number match	Glass ware wine glass
Animal match	Champagne glass
Animal doll	Eye ball glass
Cars	Whisky glass
Trailer	Food flask
Train	Water bottle
Motorcycle	Food flask
Dart magnetic board	Water vacuum flask
Optics binoculars	Binatone blender and iron
other attractive toys	Padlocks
	Extension cables
	Bulb
	Akt 16watt and 26watt spirial

Baby walker	Good com and akt led bub all sizes
Baby hanger	Florescent bulb
	Flood light
	Lamp holder
	Switch
	Plug
	Sucket
	Adapter
	Torch light all variants
	Rechargeable fan
	Rechargeable bulb
PHONE ACCESSORIES	Clippers assorted types
Sandisk flash drive 8gb,16, 32 and 64gb	Clothes Hanger
Sandisk memory card 8gb, 16, 32gb, and 64	Shoe hanger
	Umbreller
Jbl speaker	
Jbl head speaker	
Earphones	
Oraimo charger set	
Oraimo cables	
Oraimo Bluetooth	
Oraimo power bank	

Mouse	
Keyboard	
Scanners	
Harddrive	
Tv guards	
Door bell	
Other type of headset	
Other types of earpods	
Oraimo earpods	
BABIES AND BOUTIC	
Bib	
feeder	
Water bottle	
Baby clothes	
Baby hair band	White envlopes all sizes
Baby hair packer	File
Boxers	Folder
Singlet	Transparent file
Pants	10 subject notebook
Belt	12 subject notebook

Cofflinks	8 subject notebook
t-shirt	A4 paper chamex
round neck t-shirt	Double a a4 paper
socks	Notebook 60, 20, 40, 80 leaves
ironing table cover	Higher education
Hair brush	Drawing book
Dunlop slippers	Sketchpad
Crocs	Graph book
	Writing book
STATIONERIES	Drawing book
Best mathematical set	Sketch book
Campus mathematical set	Flexible ruler
Oxford mathematical set	Hard cover note book all sizes
Universe mathematical set	Gift bags all sizes
Nataraj mathematical set	Recorder flute
Nataraj eraser, sharpeners, pencils, pen, colour pencils	
Wax craypns	
Lily colour pencils big and small	
Aluminiun ruler	
Transparent rulers long and	

short	
Stylus pens	
Cellotape diferent varinats	
Casio calculator diffent variants	
Igle corrections pens	
Elris whiter board marker	
Papermanent marker	
Cardboard	
2b pencil	
Hb pencils	
Mechanical pencil	
Dictionaries	
Pencil pouch	Queen Helene lotion and cup
Pencil case	Lemon fresh lotion
Stamp ink stamp pad	Tea tree lotion
Pen different variants	Fruit of the loom aloe vera gel
Tikky 20 eraser	Cottage fresh soap
Kangaroo stapler big and small	Renew black soap
Uhu glue all sizes	Limpo ori
Water gum	Make me white lotion
Paint brush	St ives scrub

Acrylic paint	Hit the spot scrub
Water colour	Xbc scrub
Brown paper	Purity plus scrub
Id card pouch	Tree hut scrub cup
Top bond all sizes	Veet gold scrub cup
Top gum all sizes	Dr teals scrub
Envelopes brown all sizes	Just white scrub cup
	Eden scrub cup
COSMETICS	Eco style gel all sizes and variants
F&w scrub bath	Jack 5 acivator
White care bath	Gloshine gel
Boba white bath	Cream of nature edge control
Clear nature bath	Ors edge control
F&w so white, exclusive, and carrot bath	Olive edge control
	Cantu edge control
Noble white	Cream of nature hair dye
Light up bath	Dark and love hair dye
Just white bath	Face peel off mask
Veet gold bath	Cara dye red, white and gold
Aveeno bath	Above sheen spray and mouse spray
Spa fruiser bath	Ors sheen spray and mouse
Softsoap	

Johnsons bath	Veet gold sheen spray
E45 bath	Mega growth deep conditioner big and small
Irish spring bath	Mega growth leave in conditioner big and small
Olay bath	
Simple bath	Morgan hair cream yellow and black
Fruiser bath	
Vaseline bath	Gillette shaving foam
Dr teals bath	Gillette shaving cream
Easy glow bath	Gillette shaving gel
Tag bath	Xoc shampoo and conditioner
Palmolive bath	Sulfur8 shampoo
St ives bath	Vinoz shampoo and conditioner big and small
Dove bath big and small	Hair wonder shampoo
Adidas bath	Hair and scalp
Lemon fresh bath	Head and shoulder
Loreal bah	Crème of nature shampoo and conditioner
Radox bath	
Passion powder	Pantu shampoo and conditioner
Boots baby powder	Bo-16 shampoo and condition
Johnsons baby powder	L'real bath
Nycil powder	Mega growth shampoo and conditioner
Bouquet powder big and	Mega groth anti dandruff

small	shampoo
Enchanteur big and small	Olive oil shampoo and conditioner
Ponds power magic	Cream of nature shampoo and conditioner
Ponds powder	
Egyptian lotion	Dark and lovely shampoo and conditioner
Purec gold lotion	Dark and lovely leave in conditioner
Paw paw lotion and cup	
Nano lotion	Magic shaving cream and powder
pure whition big and small	After after shave
bbclaire lotion	Denim after shave
bio Claire	Nivea after shave
jergens lotion	Johnson baby lotion, bath and shampoo
olay lotion extracts lotion big and small	Boots shampoo, lotion and bath
looking good cup	Seba med lotion and soap
beauty fair cup	Aveeno shampoo, lotion and bath
lemon fresh cup	Pears lotion, bath and shampoo
skin beauty cup	Cusson bath and lotion
naturessence cup	Nycil lotion and bath
caro white lotion and cup all sizes	Baby secret oil and lotion
st ives lotion	Johnson baby oil
ct plus big and small	Baby comfort lotion and bath
	Sulfur 8 hair cream

nature secret lotion big and small	Damatol all sizes
carotone lotion and cup all sizes	So- fine hair cream all sizes
	Soul mate hair cream all sizes
Vaseline lotion all variants and sizes	Magic sporting wave hair cream and relaxer
Gluta white lotion	Apple hair cream all sizes
White glow lotion	Apple shampoo
P2g lotion	Kuza hair cream all sizes
Clear essence lotion	Swiss jardin all sizes
E45 lotion and cup	Soul mate bergamot
Neutrogena lotion	Dr miracle relaxer
Palmer cocoa butter lotion and cup	Mega growth
	Dark and lovely kit regular and super
Palmers sheer butter lotion	
Cetaphil lotion and cup	Dark and love and breakage
Cereve lotion and cup	Organic kit relaxer
Looking good lotion'	Texture my way men and women
Clear nature lotion	Beautiful beginning
F&w lotion gold, exclusive and so white	Just for me relaxer and texturizer
	Ors relaxer
Nivea all variants	
Johnsons lotion	
Miss white lotion	
	Black and white perfume and

Maxi tona lotion big and small

Nature white lotion

Easy tone lotion

Familia lotion and cup

Revlon lotion

Venus lotion and cup all variants

Pears cup cream and jelly

So white gel and cream

Lemonvate cream

Tempovate cream

Demovate cream

Movate

Skin success cream and gel

Skin doctor toner big and small

Funbact a cream

Skineal cream

Fashion fair cream and gel

Tribact

spray

Explore perfume and spray

Smart collection perfume and spray

Jadore parfume

Balila perfume

Perfect line perfume

Phylia perfume

Brown perfume

Red diamond perfume

24k perfume

Pendora perfume and spray

Senator perfume

Chairman perfume

Element perfume

Solid black perfume

New musk perfume and spray

Cosmo colour spray

Body fantasy mist

Pure black perfume

Palma rosa prfume

Active man and woman perfume

Neoskin	and spray
Karis gel vitamin c	Frank oliver mist and perfume
Veet gold toner	Amory spray
Baby face cleanser	Axe spray
Nuetrogena toner	Dove spray
Clean and clear lotion	Rexona spray
Clean and clear toner	Sure spray
Clean and clear astringent and black head	Riggs spray
	Malisia spray
Dermalislotion	Maximo spray
Peu de lune clanser	Precious spray
Skin succe cleanser	Character kid mist and roll
Beard oil	Gillette stick gel
Massage oil	Axe stick gel
Veet hair remover	Rexona stick gel
Royallux cleanser	Old spice stick gel
Rose cleanser	Nevea roll on
Kojic acid serum	Kiss roll on
Caroton serum	Brut roll
So white oil	Enchantuer roll
So white serum	Doobai roll on
F&w exclusive serum	Infinity roll

Disaar oil	Equity roll on
Bio oil all sizes	Holiday spray
Femfresh big and small	Wanna play
Bronze serum	Tony Montana spray
Pure white serum	
Caro white serum	
Sudo cream all sizes	
Beverly face cream	
Half cast face cream gold skin face cream	
Nature secrete face cream	
Bb clear faced cream	
Face wipes	
Moko spirit	
Teno nail polish remover	
Teno desolver	
Robb	
Aboniki	
Cotton wool	
Cotton pads	
Cotton balls	
Eden glycerine and rose	

water Boots glycerine and rose water	

Ekwulo C. John is a grocery "store specialist" or "supermarket guru". Who has played crucial role in assisting retailers optimize their operations and improve the entire customer experience. Throughout my career in supermarket, I have impacted my broad knowledge on various aspects that contributes to supermarket success. This includes employees consulting training on Merchandising Maven, inventory virtuoso, price strategizing, customer experience, trend spotter, supplier whisperer, tech savvy, sustainability steward, and accounting.